FIVE PILLARS
OF INVESTING

A practical guides that provide a study framework for
making informed decisions, managing risks, and
capitalizing on opportunities in the financial markets.

Albert Rogar

TABLE OF CONTENT

INTRODUCTION

CHAPTER ONE

MASTERING RESEARCH AND ANALYSIS IN INVESTMENT
A ROADMAP FOR INFORMED INVESTING
UNDERSTANDING YOUR MIND FOR SMARTER FINANCIAL DECISIONS

CHAPTER TWO

THE POWER OF DIVERSIFICATION IN INVESTMENT
ASSESSING RISK TOLERANCE
NAVIGATING THE WORLD OF INVESTMENT COSTS AND FEES

CHAPTER THREE

TIME HORIZON IN INVESTING
LONG-TERM VS. SHORT-TERM INVESTMENTS
NAVIGATING THE UPS AND DOWNS OF INVESTING

CHAPTER FOUR

SETTING AND ACHIEVING YOUR INVESTMENT GOALS
INVESTMENT STRATEGIES
MASTERING ASSET ALLOCATION

CHAPTER FIVE

INCOME AND CASH FLOW
TAX EFFICIENCY IN INVESTING
NAVIGATING THE ROAD TO RETIREMENT

CHAPTER SIX

CONCLUSION

INTRODUCTION

Investing is a powerful means to build wealth, secure your financial future, and achieve your long-term goals. However, navigating the world of investments can be a complex and challenging endeavor. To succeed in this journey, one must have a solid understanding of the fundamental principles that form the bedrock of investing. These principles often referred to as the "Pillars of Investing," provide a sturdy framework for making informed decisions, managing risks, and capitalizing on opportunities in the financial markets.

Just as the ancient Greeks built enduring structures using columns or pillars to support their architectural masterpieces, successful investors rely on these pillars to construct a sturdy foundation for their financial well-being. The Pillars of Investing encompass a range of key concepts, from risk management and asset allocation to diversification and due diligence.

In this exploration of the Pillars of Investing, we will journey through the core principles that underpin the world of finance. Each pillar represents a critical aspect of the investment landscape, offering insights into how to grow and protect your wealth while striving to achieve your financial goals. Understanding these pillars is not only advantageous but also essential for investors of all backgrounds, whether you are just starting your investment journey or are a seasoned financial expert.

Throughout this in-depth examination, we will uncover the wisdom, strategies, and time-tested approaches that have empowered investors to navigate the ever-evolving and dynamic world of finance. By the end of our journey, you will possess a comprehensive understanding of the fundamental principles of investing, enabling you to make well-informed choices, manage risks effectively, and, ultimately, build a more secure and prosperous financial future.

CHAPTER ONE

Mastering Research and Analysis in Investment

A Guide to Informed Decision-Making

Investing is not a game of chance; it's a science, and at its core is the discipline of research and analysis. The ability to gather, evaluate, and interpret information is essential for making informed investment decisions

The Role of Research and Analysis

Research and analysis are foundational to successful investing for several reasons:

❖ Informed Decision-Making: They provide the information needed to make well-informed decisions about which investments to buy, hold, or sell.

- ❖ Risk Mitigation: Effective research and analysis can help identify potential risks and opportunities, enabling investors to make adjustments to their portfolios and strategies.
- ❖ Enhanced Returns: By thoroughly researching and analyzing investments, investors can uncover undervalued assets or growth opportunities, potentially leading to higher returns.
- ❖ Long-Term Strategy: Research and analysis are essential for building and maintaining a long-term investment strategy that aligns with financial goals.

Methods of Research and Analysis

There are various methods for conducting research and analysis in the world of finance. Here are a few key approaches:

- o Fundamental Analysis: This method involves evaluating an investment's intrinsic value by examining financial statements, earnings, dividends, and overall financial health. It is commonly used for stock analysis.
- o Technical Analysis: Technical analysis focuses on past price and volume data to predict future price

movements. It involves studying charts and patterns to identify trends.

o Quantitative Analysis: Quantitative analysis uses mathematical models and statistical techniques to analyze investments. It's often used by professionals to assess portfolio risk and returns.

o Qualitative Analysis: This method involves examining non-numerical information, such as management quality, competitive advantages, and industry trends. It is commonly used in equity and company research.

o Economic Analysis: Evaluating macroeconomic factors like inflation, interest rates, and GDP growth can provide insight into the broader market and investment trends.

Tools for Research and Analysis

Several tools and resources are available to aid in the research and analysis process:

✓ Financial Statements: Annual reports, balance sheets, income statements, and cash flow statements provide valuable financial data for fundamental analysis.

- ✓ Financial News and Publications: Reputable financial news outlets and publications offer up-to-date information, market trends, and expert opinions.
- ✓ Data Analytics Software: Software and platforms like Bloomberg, Morningstar, and Fact Set provide access to vast amounts of financial data and analytical tools.
- ✓ Economic Indicators: Reports on economic factors, such as employment data, GDP growth, and consumer sentiment, can help investors assess market conditions.
- ✓ Technical Analysis Software: Software tools like Trading View and Stock Charts offer technical indicators, chart patterns, and analysis features.

Application in Investment Decision-Making

The application of research and analysis in investment decision-making involves the following steps:

- Identify Investment Opportunities: Begin by identifying potential investments based on your goals and risk tolerance.

- Gather Information: Collect relevant data, including financial statements, news, and market trends, to assess the investments.
- Analyze the Data: Apply the appropriate analysis method, such as fundamental or technical analysis, to evaluate the investments.
- Make Informed Decisions: Use your findings to make informed investment decisions, whether it's buying, holding, or selling an asset.
- Monitor and Adjust: Continuously monitor your investments and adjust your strategy based on ongoing research and analysis.

Research and analysis are integral components of successful investing. They provide the information needed to make informed investment decisions, mitigate risks, and pursue opportunities. Whether you're analyzing stocks, bonds, real estate, or any other asset class, thorough research and analysis can help you achieve your financial goals and build a robust, long-term investment strategy. By staying informed, applying various analysis methods, and utilizing the available tools and resources, you can become a more knowledgeable and confident investor.

A Roadmap for Informed Investing

Investing in the financial markets is a complex puzzle that requires careful analysis and insight. One of the crucial pieces of this puzzle is understanding economic and market indicators. These indicators are like signposts on the investment journey, providing valuable information about the state of the economy and the financial markets. In this article, we will explore what economic and market indicators are, why they matter, and how investors can use them to make informed decisions.

What Are Economic and Market Indicators?

Economic and market indicators are data points or metrics that reflect the economic health of a country, the performance of financial markets, or specific industries. These indicators are used by investors, economists, policymakers, and financial professionals to gauge the direction of the economy, identify trends, and make informed decisions.

Types of Economic Indicators

There are various types of economic indicators, each providing a different perspective on the economy. Some of the key economic indicators include:

- Gross Domestic Product (GDP): GDP measures the total economic output of a country. It's a broad indicator of the overall health of an economy.

- Unemployment Rate: The unemployment rate reveals the percentage of people who are actively seeking employment but are currently jobless. It reflects the labor market's health.

- Consumer Price Index (CPI): CPI measures the change in the prices of a basket of goods and services, providing insights into inflation.

- Producer Price Index (PPI): PPI tracks the changes in the prices received by domestic producers. It can signal future inflation or deflation trends.

- Retail Sales: Retail sales data indicate consumer spending patterns and, by extension, the health of the retail sector.

Types of Market Indicators

Market indicators, on the other hand, focus on the performance of financial markets. Some notable market indicators include:

- o Stock Market Indices: Indices like the S&P 500, Dow Jones Industrial Average, and NASDAQ Composite provide snapshots of stock market performance.
- o Bond Yields: Bond yields, such as the 10-year Treasury yield, are crucial indicators for fixed-income investors, reflecting changes in interest rates and bond prices.
- o Volatility Index (VIX): Commonly known as the "fear gauge," VIX measures the expected market volatility.
- o Volume: Trading volume reveals the number of shares or contracts traded on a given day. It indicates market interest and liquidity.
- o Market Breadth: Market breadth indicators, such as the advance-decline line, show the number of rising and falling stocks in a market, providing insights into market sentiment.

Why Economic and Market Indicators Matter

Economic and market indicators matter for several reasons:

- Informed Decision-Making: Investors use these indicators to assess the health of the economy and financial markets. This information guides investment decisions and asset allocation.
- Risk Management: By monitoring indicators, investors can identify potential risks and adjust their strategies accordingly. For example, an increase in the unemployment rate may lead to a more conservative portfolio.
- Economic Forecasting: Policymakers, businesses, and investors rely on indicators to anticipate economic trends, helping them plan for the future.
- Timing and Strategy: Market indicators can assist investors in timing their entries and exits from the market. For example, a technical indicator may signal a buy or sell opportunity.

Using Economic and Market Indicators

To use economic and market indicators effectively, consider the following:

- ✓ Stay Informed: Keep an eye on key indicators by regularly reading financial news and reports. Many financial websites and news outlets provide up-to-date information.
- ✓ Context Matters: Understand that indicators don't provide a complete picture on their own. Consider the broader economic and market context.
- ✓ Combining Indicators: Use a combination of indicators to gain a more comprehensive view. For example, GDP growth, unemployment, and consumer sentiment data can provide a well-rounded perspective on the economy.
- ✓ Historical Data: Review historical data to spot trends and patterns. This historical context can be valuable in making informed decisions.
- ✓ Be Patient: Avoid making knee-jerk reactions to a single data point. Markets and economies are complex and can be influenced by many factors.

Economic and market indicators serve as valuable tools for investors and financial professionals. By understanding and using these indicators effectively, you can make more informed decisions, manage risk, and adapt your investment strategy to changing economic and market conditions. While they don't offer crystal ball-like predictability, they provide the data and insights needed to navigate the complex world of finance with greater confidence.

Understanding Your Mind for Smarter Financial Decisions

Investing isn't just about numbers and charts; it's also about emotions and psychology. The field of behavioral finance explores how our psychological biases and emotions can influence our investment decisions. Understanding the psychology of investing is essential for making smarter financial choices and avoiding common pitfalls. In this article, we will delve into the fascinating world of investing psychology, exploring some of the key cognitive biases and emotions that can impact your investment decisions.

Emotions and Investing

Emotions play a significant role in investing. Greed, fear, excitement, and anxiety are just a few of the feelings that can influence your investment decisions. Here are some of the most common emotions encountered in the world of investing:

- ❖ Greed: This emotion can lead to overly aggressive investments and excessive risk-taking in the pursuit of high returns.
- ❖ Fear: Fear can result in panic selling during market downturns, potentially locking in losses or missing out on recovery opportunities.
- ❖ Regret: Investors often regret past decisions, which can lead to chasing returns, buying high, and selling low.
- ❖ Overconfidence: Overconfidence can lead to excessive trading and overestimating one's ability to predict the market.
- ❖ Loss Aversion: Many investors fear losses more than they value gains, causing them to hold onto losing investments for too long.
- ❖ Herd Mentality: Following the crowd can lead to buying when everyone else is buying (at high prices) and selling when everyone else is selling (at low prices).

Cognitive Biases in Investing

Cognitive biases are systematic patterns of deviation from norm or rationality in judgment. These biases can significantly impact investment decisions. Here are a few of the most prevalent cognitive biases in investing:

- o Confirmation Bias: Investors tend to seek information that confirms their existing beliefs and disregard contradictory information.
- o Anchoring: People tend to rely heavily on the first piece of information they receive (the "anchor") when making decisions, even if that information is irrelevant.
- o Availability Bias: This bias occurs when people give more weight to readily available information, such as recent events or news, rather than a more comprehensive analysis of the situation.
- o Recent Bias: Investors often overemphasize recent performance when making investment decisions, assuming that recent trends will continue.
- o Endowment Effect: People tend to ascribe more value to the things they own, leading to emotional attachment and resistance to selling investments.

Strategies for Overcoming Psychological Biases

While it's challenging to completely eliminate psychological biases, there are strategies to mitigate their impact on investment decisions:

- Emotional Awareness: Recognize and acknowledge your emotions when making investment decisions. Take a step back and assess your feelings' influence on your choices.
- Investment Plan: Develop a well-defined investment plan with clear goals, risk tolerance, and an asset allocation strategy. This can serve as a guide to prevent impulsive decisions.
- Diversification: Diversify your portfolio to spread risk and reduce the emotional attachment to individual investments.
- Long-Term Perspective: Maintain a long-term perspective. Focusing on short-term market fluctuations can lead to impulsive decisions based on emotions.
- Consult a Financial Advisor: Seeking advice from a financial advisor can provide a rational, objective perspective on your investment choices.

- Keep Informed: Stay informed about market trends, but avoid overreacting to short-term news events.

The psychology of investing is a critical aspect of making informed financial decisions. Understanding your own emotions and cognitive biases can help you navigate the complex world of investing with greater success. By developing emotional awareness, crafting a solid investment plan, and seeking professional advice when needed, you can overcome the emotional hurdles that often lead to suboptimal investment outcomes. Remember that investing is a long-term journey, and a rational, informed approach can lead to more prosperous financial results.

CHAPTER TWO

The Power of Diversification in Investment

Reducing Risk and Enhancing Returns

Investing can be an exciting and potentially lucrative endeavor, but it comes with its fair share of risks. One key strategy that seasoned investors and financial advisors often tout as a fundamental principle of sound investing is diversification. Diversification involves spreading your investments across various asset classes to reduce risk and enhance returns.

Understanding Diversification

Diversification is the practice of not putting all your eggs in one basket, so to speak. Instead of concentrating your investments in a single asset or a small number of assets, you allocate your capital across a range of different investments. This may include various asset classes such as stocks, bonds, real estate, and cash equivalents, or it can encompass different sectors and industries within those asset classes.

The Benefits of Diversification

- Risk Reduction: The primary advantage of diversification is risk reduction. By spreading your investments across different assets, you minimize the impact of a poor-performing investment on your overall portfolio. If one investment underperforms, others may help offset the losses.
- Enhanced Consistency: Diversified portfolios tend to be less volatile. They experience fewer wild swings in value, providing a smoother and more predictable investment journey. This can be especially reassuring for risk-averse investors.
- Steady Growth: Diversification allows your portfolio to capture returns from various sources. While some assets may experience temporary setbacks, others can continue to grow, providing a more balanced and steady return on investment.
- Long-Term Success: Historically, diversified portfolios have outperformed concentrated ones in the long run. Over time, the benefits of risk

reduction and consistent growth compound, resulting in a more robust financial outcome.

Implementing Diversification

Diversifying your portfolio can be achieved in several ways:

- Asset Classes: Allocate your investments across different asset classes such as equities (stocks), fixed income (bonds), real estate, and cash or cash equivalents. Each class has its unique risk and return characteristics.
- Geographic Regions: Consider investing in both domestic and international markets. By doing so, you can benefit from the performance of various economies, each with its own growth opportunities and risks.
- Sectors and Industries: Within equities, diversify by investing in a mix of sectors and industries. For example, rather than investing solely in technology stocks, consider adding positions in healthcare, consumer goods, and energy companies.
- Company Size: Diversify your equity investments across different company sizes. Combine

investments in large-cap, mid-cap, and small-cap companies to reduce concentration risk.

- Mutual Funds and Exchange-Traded Funds (ETFs): These investment vehicles offer built-in diversification. Mutual funds and ETFs pool money from multiple investors to invest in a broad range of assets or a specific index.
- Rebalancing: Regularly review and rebalance your portfolio to ensure it remains in line with your diversification strategy. Over time, changes in the value of your investments can cause your portfolio to deviate from your intended asset allocation.

Diversification is a fundamental principle of prudent investing. By spreading your investments across various asset classes, sectors, and regions, you can reduce risk and enhance the potential for returns. This strategy helps protect your portfolio from the ups and downs of individual investments and promotes a more consistent, long-term growth trajectory. While diversification does not guarantee profits or eliminate all risks, it remains a powerful tool in the hands of investors looking to build resilient and balanced portfolios.

Assessing Risk Tolerance

When it comes to investing, understanding your risk tolerance is one of the fundamental building blocks of a successful investment strategy. Risk tolerance is the degree of uncertainty or variability that an investor is willing and able to withstand in their investment portfolio. It's a crucial consideration because it guides your asset allocation, investment choices, and overall financial plan. In this article, we'll explore what risk tolerance is, why it's important, and how to assess and apply it to make informed investment decisions.

Defining Risk Tolerance

Risk tolerance is the ability and willingness of an investor to endure fluctuations in the value of their investments, particularly in response to market volatility. It's influenced by various factors, including financial objectives, investment timeline, and psychological disposition. It is not a one-size-fits-all concept and varies from one individual to another.

Why Risk Tolerance Matters

Understanding your risk tolerance is essential for several reasons:

27

- Customized Investment Approach: Your risk tolerance helps tailor your investment strategy to align with your financial goals and your comfort level with potential ups and downs in the market.
- Asset Allocation: It guides the allocation of your investments across different asset classes. A higher risk tolerance may lead to a more aggressive allocation in equities, while a lower risk tolerance may favor a more conservative mix.
- Psychological Well-being: Staying within your risk comfort zone can help reduce stress and emotional decision-making during market fluctuations, leading to more consistent, disciplined investing.
- Long-Term Success: By aligning your investments with your risk tolerance, you're more likely to stay committed to your financial plan and achieve your long-term goals.

Assessing Risk Tolerance

Several methods can help you assess your risk tolerance:

- Questionnaires: Many financial institutions and advisors offer risk tolerance questionnaires or quizzes. These assess your comfort with various investment scenarios and suggest suitable risk levels.

- Financial Goals: Your financial goals and time horizon can also guide your risk tolerance. Long-term goals may support a higher risk tolerance, while short-term goals may suggest a more conservative approach.
- Current Financial Situation: Evaluate your current financial situation, including income, expenses, and existing investments. A robust financial foundation may allow for a higher risk tolerance.
- Emotional Resilience: Consider your emotional resilience during market downturns. Can you withstand significant portfolio fluctuations without panicking or making impulsive decisions?

Applying Your Risk Tolerance

Once you've assessed your risk tolerance, apply it to your investment strategy:

- Asset Allocation: Customize your asset allocation to align with your risk tolerance. This involves determining the mix of stocks, bonds, and other assets in your portfolio.

- Diversification: Diversify your investments within each asset class to further manage risk. Diversification spreads risk across different investments, reducing the impact of a poor-performing asset.
- Regular Review: Periodically review your risk tolerance as your financial situation, goals, and emotional disposition may change over time.
- Seek Professional Guidance: Consult a financial advisor to ensure your investment strategy aligns with your risk tolerance and financial goals. Advisors can provide valuable insights and help you make informed decisions.

Risk tolerance is a critical element of investment planning. Understanding your ability and willingness to withstand market fluctuations can help you build a customized investment strategy that aligns with your financial objectives and emotional comfort. By consistently applying your risk tolerance to your investment decisions, you can increase your chances of achieving your long-term financial goals while maintaining peace of mind during periods of market volatility.

Navigating the World of Investment Costs and Fees

When it comes to investing, one of the critical factors that can significantly impact your returns and financial success is the cost associated with your investments. Understanding the various types of costs and fees involved in investment is essential to making informed decisions. In this article, we will explore the world of investment costs and fees, their significance, and how to effectively manage them to optimize your financial outcomes.

Investment Costs and Fees: The Basics

Investment costs and fees are the expenses associated with buying, holding, and selling investments. These expenses can take different forms, and understanding them is crucial for any investor. Here are some of the key types of costs and fees:

- Management Fees: These are fees paid to the investment manager or fund company for managing your investments. They are often charged as a percentage of assets under management (AUM).

- Expense Ratios: Expense ratios represent the annual operating expenses of a mutual fund or exchange-traded fund (ETF) expressed as a percentage of the fund's average net assets. This fee covers administrative and management costs.
- Sales Charges (Loads): Sales charges, or loads, are fees you pay when buying or selling mutual funds. Front-end loads are charged when purchasing, while back-end loads are levied when selling.
- Trading Commissions: These are fees charged by brokerage firms when buying or selling stocks, bonds, or other securities. They can be a flat fee or a percentage of the trade's value.
- Account Maintenance Fees: Some financial institutions charge fees for maintaining your investment accounts, such as retirement accounts or brokerage accounts.
- Taxes: Depending on the type of investments and your jurisdiction, you may be subject to capital gains taxes when selling investments.

Significance of Investment Costs and Fees

The impact of investment costs and fees on your returns cannot be understated. Here's why they matter:

- Reduced Returns: High fees can eat into your investment returns, reducing the amount of money that compounds over time.
- Erosion of Wealth: Over time, seemingly small fees can accumulate and significantly erode the value of your investments.
- 3.   Impact on Compounding: High fees hinder the power of compounding, a fundamental driver of wealth accumulation.
- Long-Term Consequences: The long-term effect of high fees can mean the difference between reaching your financial goals and falling short.

Effectively Managing Investment Costs and Fees

To optimize your investment outcomes and minimize costs and fees, consider the following strategies:

- Research and Compare: Before investing, research different investment options and compare their costs and fees. Look for low-cost funds and securities.
- Diversify: Diversification can help spread risk and reduce the potential impact of fees on your overall portfolio.
- Use Tax-Efficient Strategies: Tax-efficient investing strategies can help reduce the impact of capital gains taxes on your returns.
- Avoid High-Churn Strategies: Frequent buying and selling of investments can lead to higher trading commissions and taxes. Consider a long-term investment approach.
- Negotiate Fees: When working with financial professionals or advisors, negotiate fees and compensation structures to ensure they align with your best interests.
- Periodically Review Your Investments: Regularly review your investment portfolio to ensure it aligns with your financial goals and to make necessary adjustments.

Investment costs and fees are integral components of your financial journey. High fees can have a substantial impact on your returns over time. By understanding the various types of costs and fees, researching your investment options, and employing strategies to minimize them, you can work toward achieving your financial goals more effectively. Cost-conscious investing can lead to greater wealth accumulation and financial success.

CHAPTER THREE

Time Horizon in Investing

The Secret to Building Wealth

Time horizon is a crucial but often underestimated element in investment planning. It refers to the length of time you expect to hold an investment before needing to access your capital. Understanding your time horizon is essential because it influences your investment strategy, risk tolerance, and potential returns.

Defining Time Horizon

Your investment time horizon is the duration over which you intend to keep your investments before needing to use the funds for a specific financial goal or commitment. Time horizons can be categorized into three main types:

✓ Short-term: Typically, a short-term horizon is defined as less than three years. This includes investments for near-future goals like buying a car, taking a vacation, or covering upcoming educational expenses.

✓ Medium-term: A medium-term horizon ranges from three to ten years. It often encompasses goals like purchasing a home, funding a child's education, or preparing for a wedding.

✓ Long-term: A long-term horizon typically extends beyond ten years. It involves objectives such as retirement planning, building a nest egg, and creating generational wealth.

The Importance of Time Horizon

Understanding your time horizon is essential for several reasons:

- Risk Tolerance: Your time horizon has a direct impact on your risk tolerance. Longer time horizons can accommodate more significant fluctuations and market volatility, allowing for a potentially more aggressive investment approach.

- Investment Strategy: Your time horizon informs your investment strategy. It helps determine the mix of asset classes in your portfolio, balancing the potential for returns with risk management.

- Compounding Returns: A longer time horizon allows you to harness the power of compounding returns, which can significantly boost the growth of your investments over time.
- Financial Goals: Your time horizon aligns with your financial objectives. It ensures that your investments are tailored to meet your specific needs and timelines.

Investment Strategies by Time Horizon

Your investment strategy should be tailored to your time horizon:

- Short-Term: For short-term goals, focus on preserving capital and ensuring liquidity. Consider conservative investments like high-quality bonds, money market funds, or certificates of deposit (CDs).
- Medium-Term: A medium-term horizon allows for a balanced approach, including a mix of stocks and bonds. Diversify your portfolio to manage risk and potentially capture higher returns.

- Long-Term: With a long-term horizon, you can adopt a more aggressive strategy. A significant portion of your portfolio can be allocated to equities, aiming for long-term capital appreciation. Diversification remains important to manage risk.

Adjusting for Life Changes

Your time horizon isn't fixed; it can evolve as your life circumstances change. Periodically reassess your time horizon when major life events occur, such as marriage, children, or nearing retirement. Adjust your investment strategy to match your updated time horizon and financial goals.

Time horizon is a fundamental element of successful investing. By understanding and aligning your investments with your specific time horizon, you can tailor your strategy to achieve your financial goals. A longer time horizon offers the advantage of compounding returns and allows for a more aggressive approach, while shorter time horizons require a focus on capital preservation. Regularly reassess and adjust your investment strategy as your time horizon evolves to ensure that your portfolio remains aligned with your financial objectives.

Long-Term vs. Short-Term Investments

Choosing Your Financial Horizon

Investing is a journey with a multitude of paths, and one of the most crucial decisions you'll make is determining your investment horizon—whether to pursue long-term or short-term investment strategies. Each approach has its advantages and considerations, and understanding the key differences between them can help you make informed investment decisions aligned with your financial goals. In this article, we'll explore the distinctions, advantages, and factors to consider when choosing between long-term and short-term investments.

Long-Term Investments: The Power of Patience

Long-term investments are financial vehicles held for an extended period, typically measured in years or even decades. These investments are often associated with specific long-range financial goals, such as retirement, wealth accumulation, or generational wealth. Here's why long-term investments are so compelling:

- ➢ Compound Interest: One of the most significant advantages of long-term investments is the power of compounding. As your investments generate returns, those returns are reinvested, creating a snowball effect that can lead to substantial growth over time.
- ➢ Reduced Risk: Long-term investments are generally less susceptible to the short-term market volatility that can trigger anxiety and hasty decision-making. They can ride out market fluctuations with a focus on the bigger picture.
- ➢ Tax Benefits: In many jurisdictions, long-term investments enjoy favorable tax treatment, such as lower capital gains tax rates. This can significantly enhance your after-tax returns.
- ➢ Achieving Financial Goals: Long-term investments are well-suited for goals like retirement planning, building wealth for the future, or funding a child's education.

Short-Term Investments: Navigating the Currents

Short-term investments, on the other hand, are typically held for a shorter period, often ranging from several months to a few years. These investments are more liquid and can be used to address immediate or near-future financial needs. Here are some of the key advantages of short-term investments:

➢ Liquidity: Short-term investments are highly liquid and can be converted to cash quickly, making them ideal for meeting immediate financial obligations or opportunities.

➢ Reduced Market Risk: Short-term investments are generally less exposed to market volatility. They provide a safer harbor for capital preservation when market conditions are uncertain.

➢ Flexibility: They allow you to adjust your investment strategy or pivot to different opportunities as your financial circumstances evolve.

➢ Emergency Funds: Short-term investments can be a component of your emergency fund, providing financial security in the event of unforeseen expenses or job loss.

Choosing Your Investment Horizon

Selecting your investment horizon involves assessing your financial objectives, risk tolerance, and specific goals:

1.   Long-Term Investment Considerations:

•   Retirement Planning: If you're saving for retirement, long-term investments like a diversified portfolio of stocks and bonds can offer the potential for growth over the years.

•   Wealth Building: For building substantial wealth or generational wealth, long-term investments leverage the power of time and compounding.

•   Risk Tolerance: Long-term investors should be comfortable with the potential for short-term market fluctuations and focus on the long-range objectives.

2.   Short-Term Investment Considerations:

- Immediate Goals: Short-term investments are suited for goals like buying a home, funding a wedding, or covering educational expenses in the near future.

- Liquidity Needs: If you require quick access to your funds for emergencies or opportunities, short-term investments are a sensible choice.

- Risk Aversion: Short-term investors may prefer to limit exposure to market volatility and prioritize capital preservation.

Balancing Long-Term and Short-Term Investments

A balanced investment approach can incorporate both long-term and short-term investments to address various financial needs. For instance, you can have a long-term retirement portfolio while maintaining short-term investments to cover emergencies or upcoming expenses.

Long-term and short-term investments are both valuable tools in the investor's toolkit. Choosing between them depends on your financial goals, risk tolerance, and specific circumstances. A well-thought-out investment strategy, aligned with your chosen horizon, can help you navigate the path to financial success, whether you're building wealth for the long term or addressing immediate needs. Ultimately, the key is to make informed decisions that align with your unique financial journey.

Navigating the Ups and Downs of Investing

Investing in the financial markets can be a bit like riding a rollercoaster. Prices rise and fall, sentiments swing from optimism to pessimism, and economic conditions constantly evolve. To make informed investment decisions, it's essential to understand market cycles. Market cycles are recurring patterns of economic and financial behavior that influence asset prices and investment strategies. In this article, we will delve into the concept of market cycles, explore their different phases, and discuss strategies for navigating these fluctuations successfully.

The Four Phases of Market Cycles

Market cycles typically go through four distinct phases, each characterized by its unique economic and market conditions:

- ✓ Expansion (Recovery): This phase marks the beginning of an upswing. Economic growth is robust, and asset prices rise. Investors are optimistic, and the employment rate is often high. Companies report strong earnings, and consumer spending is on the rise.
- ✓ Peak (Euphoria): In this phase, the market reaches its zenith. Asset prices soar to all-time highs, and investor confidence is at its peak. Companies report record profits, and everyone seems to be investing. However, it's often during this phase that signs of excessive speculation and overvaluation emerge.
- ✓ Contraction (Recession): This phase sees the market correcting as economic growth slows down. Asset prices begin to fall, and investor sentiment turns cautious. Companies report declining earnings, and unemployment rates rise. Fear and uncertainty start to dominate the market.
- ✓ Trough (Depression): The market reaches its lowest point during this phase. Asset prices are at their nadir, and investor sentiment is pessimistic. Companies report weak earnings, and economic conditions appear grim. It is at this point that

savvy investors often begin to see opportunities and re-enter the market.

Navigating Market Cycles

Navigating market cycles can be challenging, but there are strategies to help you make more informed investment decisions:

- Diversification: Maintain a diversified portfolio across various asset classes. Diversification can help mitigate the impact of market fluctuations in one particular asset or sector.
- Asset Allocation: Adjust your asset allocation based on the current phase of the market cycle. During periods of expansion, consider a slightly more aggressive allocation, and during contractions, a more conservative one.
- Risk Management: Implement risk management techniques, such as setting stop-loss orders or using options to protect against major losses.
- Buy and Hold: For long-term investors, a buy-and-hold strategy may be appropriate. This approach involves holding onto investments through market fluctuations, relying on the long-term upward trend of the markets.

- Research and Analysis: Continuously assess the economic and market indicators to make well-informed investment decisions. Fundamental and technical analysis can provide insights into market direction.
- Stress Testing: Consider the worst-case scenarios for your investments and develop a plan for how you would respond. This preparedness can reduce emotional reactions during market volatility.
- Consult a Financial Advisor: Seeking advice from a financial advisor or investment professional can be invaluable during challenging market conditions. They can provide guidance based on your financial goals and risk tolerance.

Understanding market cycles is a key aspect of successful investing. These cycles are natural, and while they can be challenging, they also present opportunities for those who know how to navigate them. By employing diversified portfolios, effective risk management, and a disciplined approach to investing, you can better weather the fluctuations and make the most of the opportunities that market cycles offer. Whether you're a short-term trader or a long-term investor, a keen awareness of market cycles can be a valuable tool in your investment arsenal.

CHAPTER FOUR

Setting and Achieving Your Investment Goals

A Path to Financial Success

Investing is not just about putting your money to work; it's about realizing your financial aspirations and securing your future. Setting clear investment goals is the foundation of a successful investment journey.

The Importance of Investment Goals

- Clarity and Direction: Investment goals give your financial journey a clear direction. They help you focus on what you want to achieve, whether it's funding your retirement, buying a home, or paying for your child's education.
- Motivation: Clear goals can serve as powerful motivators. When you have a specific financial

target in mind, you're more likely to stay committed to your investment plan and overcome challenges along the way.

- Planning and Strategy: Investment goals are the basis for creating a comprehensive investment plan. Your goals determine the type of investments, risk tolerance, and asset allocation that will be most suitable for your needs.

- Measuring Progress: Having well-defined goals allows you to track your progress. You can see how your investments are performing relative to your objectives and make necessary adjustments.

Defining Investment Goals

✓ Short-Term Goals: These are typically goals you aim to achieve within the next one to three years. Examples include building an emergency fund, saving for a vacation, or purchasing a new car.

✓ Medium-Term Goals: Medium-term goals fall in the range of three to ten years. Examples include saving for a down payment on a home, funding your child's education, or starting a business.

✓ Long-Term Goals: Long-term goals extend beyond ten years and are often associated with major life events, such as retirement planning, generational

wealth creation, or achieving financial
independence.

Prioritizing and Quantifying Your Goals

To set and achieve your investment goals effectively,
follow these steps:

- ✓ Prioritize: List your goals in order of importance.
  For instance, funding your child's education might
  take precedence over a luxury vacation.
- ✓ Quantify: Assign specific, quantifiable targets to
  your goals. Rather than a vague "saving for
  retirement," aim for a particular sum you want to
  have in your retirement fund.
- ✓ Timeframe: Set a realistic timeframe for each
  goal. For example, if you plan to buy a home in
  five years, you can calculate how much you need
  to save annually.
- ✓ 4.   Risk Tolerance: Consider your risk tolerance
  for each goal. Short-term goals might call for more
  conservative investments, while long-term goals
  can accommodate higher risk for potentially
  higher returns.

Strategies for Achieving Investment Goals

- Regular Contributions: Consistently contribute to your investment accounts to ensure that you are making progress toward your goals.
- Diversify: Diversification helps manage risk. Spread your investments across different asset classes to reduce exposure to market volatility.
- Review and Adjust: Periodically review your investment portfolio to ensure it aligns with your financial goals and risk tolerance. Make adjustments as necessary.
- Seek Professional Guidance: Consult a financial advisor to receive personalized advice and guidance tailored to your unique goals and circumstances.
- Stay Disciplined: Stick to your investment plan, even in the face of market fluctuations and economic uncertainty.

Setting clear and achievable investment goals is the cornerstone of financial success. By defining your goals, quantifying them, and prioritizing them, you can build a comprehensive investment plan that guides your financial journey. Regular contributions, diversification, and disciplined commitment to your plan are keys to realizing your investment goals. Whether you're saving for short-term needs or long-term aspirations, a well-thought-out investment strategy will help you achieve your financial objectives and secure your future.

Investment Strategies

Investing is both an art and a science, and choosing the right investment strategies is essential for achieving your financial goals. Whether you're aiming for short-term gains, building wealth over time, or securing a comfortable retirement, a well-thought-out investment strategy can be your roadmap to success. In this article, we'll explore various investment strategies, their advantages and disadvantages, and how to select the approach that best aligns with your unique financial objectives.

The Role of Investment Strategies

Investment strategies are systematic approaches that guide how you allocate your capital and make investment decisions. They play a crucial role in achieving your financial goals for several reasons:

- Risk Management: Effective investment strategies help manage risk by diversifying your portfolio, spreading risk across various asset classes, and adapting to different market conditions.
- Return Optimization: These strategies are designed to optimize returns, ensuring that your investments are well-suited to your risk tolerance and financial objectives.
- Consistency: Investment strategies provide a consistent framework for making investment decisions, reducing the likelihood of impulsive actions driven by market fluctuations.
- Adaptability: They can be tailored to your investment time horizon, risk tolerance, and specific financial goals.

Common Investment Strategies

There are various investment strategies to choose from, each with its own advantages and disadvantages. Here are some of the most popular ones:

- Buy and Hold: This strategy involves buying investments and holding them for the long term, often years or even decades. It is based on the belief that, over time, markets tend to rise, and short-term fluctuations are less relevant.
- Dollar-Cost Averaging: With this strategy, you invest a fixed amount of money at regular intervals, regardless of market conditions. It reduces the impact of market volatility and can potentially lead to better long-term returns.
- Value Investing: Value investors seek undervalued assets that are trading below their intrinsic value. The goal is to buy low and sell high when the market recognizes the true worth of the investment.
- Growth Investing: Growth investors focus on assets with the potential for high, above-average returns. These investments are typically in companies with strong growth prospects.
- Income Investing: This strategy focuses on generating a consistent stream of income, often through dividends, interest payments, or rental income. It's suitable for investors seeking regular cash flow.

- Momentum Investing: Momentum investors buy assets that have been performing well recently with the belief that they will continue to do so. It's a strategy that aims to ride trends in the market.

Selecting the Right Investment Strategy

Choosing the right investment strategy depends on your financial goals, risk tolerance, and time horizon. Here are some steps to help you decide:

- Set Clear Goals: Determine your financial objectives, whether they involve wealth preservation, income generation, or long-term growth.
- Assess Risk Tolerance: Evaluate your comfort with market fluctuations and your willingness to accept risk for potentially higher returns.
- Consider Time Horizon: The length of time you plan to hold your investments will influence your choice of strategy.
- Diversify: Regardless of your chosen strategy, diversification remains essential. Spread your

investments across different asset classes to manage risk.

- Regular Review: Periodically assess your strategy and portfolio to ensure they remain aligned with your financial goals. Make adjustments as necessary.
- Seek Professional Advice: Consult a financial advisor to receive personalized guidance that aligns with your unique circumstances and goals.

Investment strategies are the cornerstone of successful investing. By selecting an approach that aligns with your financial goals, risk tolerance, and time horizon, you can optimize your returns while managing risk. Regardless of the strategy you choose, consistent commitment, diversification, and periodic review are keys to achieving your financial objectives. Whether you're looking to preserve your wealth, generate income, or build long-term growth, a well-structured investment strategy can guide you along the path to financial success.

Mastering Asset Allocation

Asset allocation is one of the fundamental principles of prudent investing. It involves dividing your investment portfolio among different asset classes, such as stocks, bonds, and cash, to optimize returns while managing risk. A well-crafted asset allocation strategy can be the cornerstone of a successful investment plan. In this article, we'll delve into the concept of asset allocation, explore its importance, and discuss strategies for creating an effective asset allocation plan.

The Importance of Asset Allocation

Asset allocation is vital for several reasons:

- Risk Management: Diversifying across asset classes can help mitigate risk. When one asset class underperforms, others may provide stability or growth, reducing the overall impact on your portfolio.
- Optimizing Returns: Asset allocation aims to strike a balance between risk and return. It allows you to capture the potential returns of various asset classes while spreading risk.
- Matching Goals and Risk Tolerance: Asset allocation can be tailored to your investment goals and risk tolerance. A well-structured allocation aligns with your financial objectives,

whether they involve wealth preservation, income generation, or long-term growth.

- Adaptability: Asset allocation can be adjusted over time to accommodate changing financial goals, market conditions, and personal circumstances.

Types of Asset Classes

Asset allocation generally involves three primary asset classes:

- Equities (Stocks): Stocks represent ownership in companies. They tend to offer the highest potential returns but also come with higher risk due to market volatility.
- Fixed Income (Bonds): Bonds are debt securities issued by governments, corporations, or municipalities. They provide regular interest payments and are typically considered lower risk compared to stocks.
- Cash and Cash Equivalents: Cash and cash equivalents include money market funds and short-term government bonds. They offer liquidity and stability but tend to have lower returns.

Creating an Effective Asset Allocation

Designing an effective asset allocation plan involves several key steps:

- Identify Your Goals: Start by defining your investment objectives. Are you saving for retirement, a home purchase, or a child's education? Your goals will shape your asset allocation.
- Assess Your Risk Tolerance: Determine your risk tolerance by considering your financial situation, investment timeline, and comfort with market fluctuations. Are you willing to accept higher risk for the potential of higher returns, or do you prefer more stability?
- Diversify: Diversification is the core of asset allocation. Allocate your investments across different asset classes to spread risk. The precise allocation will depend on your goals and risk tolerance.
- Consider Investment Horizon: The length of time you plan to hold your investments should influence your asset allocation. Long-term

investors may have a higher allocation to stocks, while those with shorter horizons may opt for a more conservative allocation.

- Monitor and Rebalance: Regularly review your portfolio to ensure it aligns with your asset allocation strategy. Market fluctuations can cause deviations from your intended allocation, so rebalance as needed.
- Seek Professional Advice: Consulting with a financial advisor can be valuable, especially if you're unsure about your asset allocation strategy or have complex financial goals.

Asset allocation is a cornerstone of successful investing. By spreading your investments across different asset classes and tailoring your allocation to your goals and risk tolerance, you can optimize returns while managing risk. Creating an effective asset allocation strategy is a dynamic process that evolves with your financial journey. Regular review and adjustments ensure your portfolio stays in line with your investment objectives, allowing you to pursue financial success with confidence and clarity.

CHAPTER FIVE

Income and Cash Flow

The Building Blocks of Financial Success

Income and cash flow are the lifeblood of your financial well-being. Understanding these fundamental concepts and how they interconnect is crucial for managing your finances, achieving your goals, and building financial security.

Understanding Income

Income is the money you receive from various sources, such as employment, investments, business activities, and government benefits. It is the foundation upon which your financial life is built. Key points to consider about income include:

- Types of Income: Income can be categorized into several types, including earned income (salaries and wages), passive income (investments and real estate), and portfolio income (dividends and interest).

- Gross vs. Net Income: Gross income is the total earnings before taxes and deductions, while net income is what remains after taxes and other deductions have been subtracted.
- Fixed and Variable Income: Some income sources are predictable and stable, while others may be variable or irregular.
- Diversification: Having multiple sources of income can provide stability and security, as it reduces reliance on a single income stream.

Significance of Income

Income plays a pivotal role in shaping your financial well-being:

- Covering Expenses: Your income is what allows you to meet your daily living expenses, pay bills, and fund your lifestyle.
- Building Wealth: A portion of your income can be saved and invested to grow your wealth over time.

- Emergency Fund: Income helps you establish and maintain an emergency fund, providing a safety net for unexpected expenses.
- Meeting Financial Goals: Income is essential for achieving financial goals, whether it's buying a home, funding education, or planning for retirement.

Understanding Cash Flow

Cash flow, on the other hand, is the movement of money in and out of your accounts over a specified period. It reflects how well your income covers your expenses and financial obligations. Key points about cash flow include:

- Positive vs. Negative Cash Flow: Positive cash flow occurs when your income exceeds your expenses, leaving a surplus that can be saved or invested. Negative cash flow happens when expenses exceed income, potentially leading to financial stress.
- Cash Flow Management: Effective cash flow management involves budgeting, tracking expenses, and ensuring that your income is sufficient to cover your financial obligations.

- Liquidity: Cash flow represents the liquidity of your financial situation, indicating how easily you can access money when needed.

Significance of Cash Flow

Cash flow is crucial for your financial health:

- Financial Stability: Positive cash flow ensures you can meet your financial obligations and maintain stability in your daily life.
- Debt Management: It allows you to manage debts effectively, reducing the risk of falling into a debt spiral.
- Investment Opportunities: Positive cash flow provides the means to invest and build wealth, while negative cash flow can limit your investment capacity.
- Emergency Preparedness: It helps establish an emergency fund and ensures you have funds available for unexpected expenses.

Balancing Income and Cash Flow

Achieving a balance between income and cash flow is essential for financial success:

- Budgeting: Create a budget to manage your expenses and ensure that your income is sufficient to cover them.
- Emergency Fund: Establish an emergency fund to handle unexpected expenses, ensuring that your cash flow remains stable.
- Debt Management: Manage debts wisely to avoid negative cash flow and maintain financial stability.
- Savings and Investments: Allocate a portion of your income to savings and investments to grow your wealth and secure your financial future.

Income and cash flow are the foundations of your financial life. Understanding how they work, managing them effectively, and striking a balance between them are essential for building financial security and achieving your goals. By wisely managing your income and cash flow, you can navigate the financial complexities of daily life and prepare for a more secure and prosperous future.

Tax Efficiency in Investing

Maximizing Returns and Minimizing Liabilities

When it comes to investing, the focus is often on achieving the highest possible returns. However, an equally important aspect of successful investing is minimizing tax liabilities. Tax efficiency is the art of structuring your investments in a way that maximizes after-tax returns. In this article, we'll explore the importance of tax efficiency, strategies for optimizing it, and the benefits it offers to investors.

Understanding Tax Efficiency

Tax efficiency in investing refers to the ability to minimize the impact of taxes on your investment returns. It involves making strategic decisions about the types of accounts in which you hold investments, the timing of buying and selling assets, and the choice of investments themselves.

The Importance of Tax Efficiency

Tax efficiency is crucial for several reasons:

- Preserving Wealth: High taxes can erode your investment gains over time. Minimizing taxes helps preserve your wealth and achieve your financial goals more effectively.
- Boosting Returns: Reducing the tax drag on your investments can lead to higher after-tax returns. This can significantly impact your long-term wealth accumulation.
- Enhancing Cash Flow: Efficient tax strategies can help you generate more income from your investments while keeping your tax liability in check.
- Risk Management: Minimizing taxes can reduce the need to take on additional risk to achieve your financial goals.

Strategies for Tax Efficiency

- Tax-Advantaged Accounts: Take full advantage of tax-advantaged accounts like 401(k)s, IRAs, and HSAs. Contributions to these accounts are often tax-deductible, and investment gains can grow tax-deferred or tax-free.

- Asset Location: Place investments with higher tax implications, such as bonds or actively managed funds, in tax-advantaged accounts. Equities, which are more tax-efficient, can be held in taxable accounts.
- Tax-Loss Harvesting: Offset capital gains by selling investments with capital losses to minimize your tax liability.
- Holding Period: Long-term investments generally enjoy lower capital gains tax rates than short-term investments. Consider holding assets for the long term to benefit from this.
- Tax-Efficient Investments: Choose investments that are tax-efficient, such as index funds or ETFs, which tend to generate fewer taxable events than actively managed funds.
- Gifting and Inheritance Planning: Be mindful of the tax implications of gifts and inheritance. Proper estate planning can reduce potential estate taxes.

Benefits of Tax Efficiency

- Increased Wealth: Minimizing taxes allows your investments to grow more rapidly, increasing your overall wealth.
- Lower Stress: Effective tax planning reduces financial stress and the anxiety of tax season.
- Improved Cash Flow: Efficient tax strategies can lead to more income in your pocket, enhancing your financial stability.
- Enhanced Retirement: Tax efficiency can help ensure your retirement savings go further, providing greater financial security in your later years.
- Risk Mitigation: Lowering your tax liability can reduce the need to take on excessive risk in your investments.

Tax efficiency in investing is a critical aspect of achieving your financial goals. It not only helps you preserve your wealth and boost your returns but also provides peace of mind and enhanced financial security. By strategically employing tax-advantaged accounts, asset location, and other tax-efficient strategies, you can minimize your tax liability and enjoy the full benefits of your hard-earned investments. Working with a financial advisor or tax professional can further assist you in optimizing your tax efficiency strategy.

Navigating the Road to Retirement

Retirement, often seen as the golden years of life, represents a period of newfound freedom, relaxation, and the pursuit of lifelong dreams. Yet, the key to enjoying a fulfilling retirement lies in careful planning. Retirement planning is a comprehensive strategy that encompasses financial, lifestyle, and health considerations. In this article, we will delve into the world of retirement planning, exploring its significance, key components, and how to embark on the journey towards a secure and satisfying retirement.

The Significance of Retirement Planning

Retirement planning is essential for several reasons:

- Financial Security: It ensures that you have the financial resources to maintain your desired lifestyle during retirement.
- Longevity: With increasing life expectancy, planning for a retirement that could last decades is crucial.
- Easing Transitions: Thoughtful planning can ease the transition from a full-time career to a more leisurely and fulfilling retirement.
- Fulfillment: Retirement planning allows you to explore new interests, travel, and spend quality time with loved ones.

Key Components of Retirement Planning

- Financial Planning: This includes determining your retirement income needs, creating a budget, saving and investing, and optimizing tax efficiency. Consider retirement accounts like 401(k)s, IRAs, and Social Security benefits.

- Lifestyle Planning: Decide how you want to spend your retirement. Will you travel, pursue hobbies, or engage in volunteer work? Lifestyle planning helps you define your goals and aspirations.

- Healthcare Planning: Consider your healthcare needs in retirement, including Medicare and supplemental insurance, long-term care, and end-of-life preferences.

- Estate Planning: Ensure that your assets are distributed according to your wishes and minimize the tax burden on your heirs.

Getting Started with Retirement Planning

- Assess Your Current Situation: Determine your current financial status, including your savings, investments, debts, and expenses.

- Set Clear Goals: Define your retirement goals. How do you envision your retirement lifestyle, and what are your financial targets?

- Create a Budget: Establish a budget that outlines your anticipated expenses in retirement and how you plan to cover them.

- Maximize Retirement Accounts: Contribute to retirement accounts like 401(k)s and IRAs. Take advantage of employer matching contributions if available.

- Diversify Investments: Build a diversified investment portfolio that aligns with your risk tolerance and financial goals.

- Consult a Financial Advisor: Seek the guidance of a financial advisor to create a personalized retirement plan and receive expert advice.

- Regularly Review and Adjust: Periodically review your retirement plan to ensure it remains on track, and make adjustments as necessary.

Retirement planning is a vital part of securing your financial future and realizing your dreams during your golden years. Whether you are approaching retirement or have many years to go, thoughtful planning is essential. By taking a proactive approach to financial, lifestyle, healthcare, and estate planning, you can pave the way for a retirement filled with financial security, fulfillment, and the freedom to enjoy life on your own terms. The journey to a successful retirement begins with a well-crafted plan, and the time to start is now.

CHAPTER SIX

CONCLUSION

The pillars of investing are the fundamental principles that underpin the world of finance and guide investors toward successful wealth-building and financial security. These pillars provide a sturdy framework for making informed decisions, managing risks, and capitalizing on opportunities in the ever-evolving financial markets.

Diversification, the first pillar, takes asset allocation a step further. It emphasizes spreading investments within each asset class to further reduce risk. Diversification allows investors to mitigate the impact of poor-performing assets and capture gains from others, ultimately leading to a more balanced and resilient portfolio

Another pillar, Risk Management, emphasizes the importance of understanding and mitigating risks associated with investments. Successful investors are those who strike a balance between risk and reward, diversify their portfolios, and remain prepared for the inevitable fluctuations in the market. By prudently managing risk, investors can safeguard their capital and secure their financial future.

Investment strategy, which is another pillar, underscores the significance of strategically distributing investments across various asset classes, such as stocks, bonds, and real estate. Proper asset allocation helps investors achieve a balance between risk and return, aligning their portfolios with their financial goals and risk tolerance. It is a critical component in constructing a resilient and profitable investment strategy.

Research and analysis, which is another pillar, underscores the necessity of thorough research and analysis before making investment decisions. Conducting due diligence involves evaluating potential investments, understanding their fundamentals, and scrutinizing their historical performance. It's the foundation for informed investment choices and minimizing the risk of making hasty or uninformed decisions.

As we explore these pillars, we come to appreciate that investing is not a one-size-fits-all endeavor. Each individual's financial goals, risk tolerance, and circumstances are unique, making it imperative to personalize investment strategies. Successful investors combine these pillars to create a customized and effective investment plan tailored to their specific needs.

In the ever-evolving landscape of finance, these pillars are enduring and timeless, guiding investors through both bull and bear markets. They provide wisdom, strategies, and time-tested approaches that empower investors to navigate the financial complexities of daily life and achieve long-term financial success.

In embracing these pillars, investors are better equipped to construct a sturdy foundation for their financial well-being. By understanding risk, optimizing asset allocation, diversifying wisely, and conducting due diligence, investors can navigate the complexities of the investment world, ultimately building a more secure and prosperous financial future. In the dynamic world of finance, the pillars of investing serve as steadfast companions, offering valuable insights and guidance for all those who seek to harness their power on the path to financial success.

www.ingramcontent.com/pod-product-compliance
Lightning Source LLC
Chambersburg PA
CBHW010722110626
46523CB00046B/712